NEXT LEVEL BEAUTIFUL
POSSESSING BEAUTY BEYOND PAIN

TAWANDA LA'SHUN USHER

LIFE TO LEGACY

Next Level Beautiful:
Possessing Beauty Beyond Pain
Copyright © 2017 by Tawanda La'Shun Usher
ISBN-13 978-1-947288-12-6
ISBN-10 1-947288-12-1

All rights reserved solely by the author under international Copyright Law. Except where designated, the author certifies that all contents are original and do not infringe upon the legal rights of any other person or work. No part of this book may be reproduced in any form without the expressed written permission of the author and publisher. The views expressed in this book are not necessarily those of the publisher.

Scripture marked KJV are take from the authorized King James Version. Scripture marked **NIV** are taken from the New International Version®, **NIV**® Copyright © 1973, 1978, 1984, 2011 by Biblica, Inc.® Used by permission. All rights reserved worldwide. Scripture marked **MSG** are taken from The Message. Copyright © 1993, 1994, 1995, 1996, 2000, 2001, 2002. Used by permission of NavPress Publishing Group.

Printed in the United States

10 9 8 7 6 5 4 3 2 1

Cover design by: Traneisha Y. Jones

Personal Stylist: Charly King

Hair Stylist: Venita Graves

Cover photo by: Point and Click Photography

> Published by: Life To Legacy, LLC
> 15255 S. 94th Ave, 5th Floor
> Orland Park, IL 60462
> 877-267-7477
> Life2legacybooks@att.net

Table of Contents

Acknowledgments	4
Foreword	6
Foreword II	7
Next Level Beautiful	9
1. Battle of the Past	12
2. Battle of the Tongue	22
3. Battle of the Flesh	28
4. Battle of Temptation	32
5. Battle of Fear	37
6. Battle of the Spirit	41
7. Battle of the Mind	45
8. Battle of Insecurity	50
9. Battle of People	54
10. Battle of Poverty	60
11. Battle of Procrastination	66
12. Battle of the Future	71
13. Blessed Beyond the Battle	76

Acknowledgments

With special thanks to some special people, without whom this project would not have been written. I am forever in their debt for the lessons they have taught and the encouragement they have given.

Bishop E. L. Usher, my anointed husband, pastor and friend. Thank you for your enduring love and support; physically, mentally, financially and emotionally. You have been my biggest fan and supporter during this project and within my life. You are my mentor, my teacher and my closet friend. I am in awe of your strength and wisdom. You are truly a Mega-Man with a Mega-Ministry serving a Mega-God. Your love is true, honest and forever. You have made my dreams and aspirations come true. I am forever grateful for your love and support.

Claudia Boyd-Colter, my mother and friend. Thank you for imparting so much of your wisdom and tough love. You have nurtured and shaped my life. Thank you for laboring with me and believing in me.

Ambassador Sophia Ruffin, your friendship have been priceless. You have proven yourself to be authentic, reliable and very valuable. Thank you for pushing me beyond regular boundaries. You have labored with me and turned rough writing into polished text. Blessings and Favor rest upon you.

To every teacher, business partner, family member and friend – I am forever grateful that our lives crossed paths. You have made me a better person. You are loved and appreciated.

Ambria McDonald – The late and last minute edits and conversations during this project has blessed my life. You are truly a blessed and brilliant young lady. Thank you for always saying, "Yes!"

Traneisha Jones – Thank you for creating this amazing design for the book cover. You are simply incredible.

To my Editor and Publisher, whose unseen touch has enriched every page of this manuscript, thank you for keeping me focused and moving forward. I am forever grateful.

Foreword

I believe the biggest crime in our society is the same crime in the Christian world and that is Identity Theft. The enemy (Satan) has robbed the people of God of their true identity. He doesn't want you to know just how beautiful you really are. You were made in the image and likeness of God Himself and you were created to reflect who He is in your life. When you begin to let go of your past and embrace who God says you are you will discover your Next Level Beautiful.

Tawanda La'Shun Usher captures the pure essence of these biblical truths. As she helps you to uncover and expose those areas of your life that you have battled with and that has robbed you of your true identity; you will walk away empowered and victorious. You will truly discover growing from "Glory to Glory," the unveiling of whom God says you are. Get ready to experience Next Level Beautiful now!

–Apostle Cynthia Brazelton

Foreword II

Many people have the desire of going to the Next Level, and this statement is one that does not discriminate. It's in our DNA to strive for more, by having an inner desire of advancing, progressing, and excelling to the next level. Although each next level status varies from person to person, it's a momentum word that has the ability to thrust you from one place to the next. This desire is not bound by the four walls of the church, and has the ability to break out in the life of any individual open to receiving their next level.

Next Level Beautiful, approaches the next level from a unique perspective. This book addresses battles that we have either faced, or will face as we continue to grow. *Next Level Beautiful* approaches battles from a scriptural, transparent foundation that demonstrates wisdom from a spiritual level as well as from experience.

It clarifies the problems we face, as well as provide powerful, empowering, enriching solutions. It is an "in your face" read that leaves you wanting more. After you complete this book, you will be ready to soar into your next level, leaving all barriers behind, as you thrust into your new. *Next Level Beautiful* confronts the ugly battles we face, while offering us divine insight on how to grow into the beautiful creatures ordained by God. I highly recommend this book, and declare that you will complete this book with an impartation for your *Next Level Beautiful*.

–Sophia Ruffin
Founder of Sophia Ruffin Ministries
Author of *From Point Guard to Prophet*

NEXT LEVEL BEAUTIFUL
POSSESSING BEAUTY BEYOND PAIN

Show me your struggle and I'll show you your victory. Every person has one. We are human and not exempt from the different battles that impact our lives. Whether you want to admit it or not, you are in the fight of your life. All bets are off! It's time to roll up your sleeves and take back what has tried to take you.

As you embark on your journey to Next Level Beautiful, the pages that follow will challenge you, encourage you, but most of all, they will free you from everything hindering you from obtaining the next chapter of your life.

Each chapter has been specifically designed with you in mind. You will find practical and applicable words of wisdom, a prayer for each layer that you will expose, and a space where you will make a declaration by declaring what's next for your life. Next Level Beautiful will come from a place of great battles fought and the victories that you won. Before reading another word, you must first confess, "I Am A Champion!"

As you journey to Next Level Beautiful, understand that your words are going to be very vital and powerful for your path forward. What you say, you shall have and what you say, you will become. Next Level Beautiful is more than words on a page; it is who you are. *Arise, shine; for your light is come, and the glory of the Lord is risen upon you... to give unto them beauty for ashes"* (Isaiah 60:1, 61:3).

First, we must pause and look into our life, our issues, and our struggles, both past and present. In order to understand the journey, you must reset your mind. It is impossible to thrust forward while looking back. The battles that you have tried to conceal are actually not hidden at all. You have lived with them, fought through them, and now you must aim to master them – battles of the past, present and perhaps the future.

You have silenced the battles in public and struggled with them in private. You have decreed and declared breakthrough over everything but haven't addressed the hidden issues. You have labeled it "your battle" and accepted it as a part of your life. You take it on vacation and allow it to operate whenever it decides to. Your life has become a comfortable home for it; but today, we send eviction letters and we post "vacate now" notices. Is this a spiritual or a natural battle? I say to you, "Yes. It is both!" You cannot address what you are not willing to arrest. We are not asking the battle to stop; we are ending the relationship altogether. The Bible says, "The battle is not yours, it is the Lord's."

In reality, this battle has continued because you have not taken authority over it. We have made excuses and have made others accept it as a part of who we are. That day is over. Today, we face it, address it, expose it and in prayer, position to heal it. In order to address every area of the battles you struggle with, we must first deal with one of the greatest areas that affect us the most, The Battle of the Past. Welcome to Next Level Beautiful.

One

BATTLE OF THE PAST

Transparency produces healing and healing produces wholeness. I personally wish this chapter was last in the book. Because of the scars that I must share, it makes me very vulnerable. But I can't ask for beauty while hiding ashes. I too, want to be completely free of my past and the pain that was produced from it. As I reminisce, I can remember very ugly days of my childhood; never fitting in, always the oddball, no talent, not pretty enough, not smart enough, or built perfect enough, So I thought!

These are real scars that I allowed life to create for me that I subconsciously carried. I began to wear this pain like a winter coat in the summer time. It was hot, heavy, too large and very uncomfortable. It didn't fit into the season of my life that I was being called into, but I couldn't shake it, and I couldn't pull it off. It felt as if it owned me. It wouldn't let me go forward because the past wasn't done trying to rob and rape me out of my future. It was relentless, constantly reminding me that it controlled me. I woke up daily seeing this battle in a shaded and blurred mirror. It spoke directly to me as though it was my middle name.

Why did I allow the pain of my past to control and manipulate me? It had a grip around my conscience like a heart surgeon doing a transplant to save a life. I wanted to be free from it. I needed to sign the divorce papers of my past and then burn them. Not only burn them, but take the ashes to the Atlantic Ocean and scatter them. It was more than a message in a bottle that I needed to release; I needed to be healed from the scars that had crippled and handicapped my growth.

Believing the one person I trusted most, she let me down. She said ugly things to me. She called me names that cut deeply. She didn't really love me or value the gifts and treasures inside of me. She… was me. I rehearsed to myself the countless mistakes I had chosen to make in the name of love. What love? That wasn't love it was deep pain.

I can remember at the age of fifteen, looking into the mirror, staring at myself saying repetitively, "Nobody really loves me." The tears that I cried was like a running faucet with no control. I was releasing tears of pain, low self-esteem, and insecurity. I grew up with the love of both parents and couldn't understand why I felt so empty and alone. It was an inside job that needed to be fixed. I thought by releasing the tears it would free my soul and the black sheep that was riding on my back would release me. I only discovered that the black sheep wasn't riding me, it lived inside of me. It slept with me, ate with me, rode with me, I couldn't shake it off no matter what I tried. My desire was freedom but the battle of the past only mission was to keep me locked in a jail cell that had no keys.

I didn't want to face the demon that wrestled me down daily, but I couldn't deny that it controlled me. It was stronger and more powerful than anything that I had faced and it consistently reminded me of its grip by controlling my personal perspective of myself. My past failures was built with walls of pain and agony and bolted with bars made of steel.

Thinking back on this particular dark and shaded day, I can still remember the effect it had on my mind, thoughts, and vision. In the back room of my mother's house, I can clearly remember daunting voices of depression and sadness steering me to a place of despair and darkness. That feeling of heaviness and no self-worth begin to chase me. It spoke clearly to me by giving me deadly instructions on how to end my life. Because of the years I allowed this darkness to feed me, it was easy to accept the invitation. It was a voice of pure anxiousness and peer pressure pushing me to move forward with the plan quickly. That voice of darkness spoke heroic lies in my ears, "Be brave for once in your life, open up that shaving razor and go as deep into your vein. You will be finally free." The spirit of suicide knew that freedom was my desire and it imitated freedom by trying to play on my emotions.

The private tears of my pain had been bottled up for so long that jars of them were filled and running over. As I begin to yield a yes to the dark-side of suicide and submit to the voice that soothed my pain, I begin to slash at my wrist. One cut after the next, and with every slash my drive to live and breathe became my savior. Scriptures from my childhood memories began to flow through my mind; Jeremiah 29:11"For I know the plans that I have for you, declares the LORD, "plans to prosper you and not to harm you, plans to give you hope and a future. As that Scripture played like a movie on a big screen in my mind, tears began to wash away the blood that the razor caused. I fell to my knees and this time, I cried out to God from my heart. The pain that I felt began to fade because my passion to embrace what God had in store for my life was louder than the pain.

As I reminisce on my past, I can still see the scars but can no longer feel the pain. It reminds me of where I was but what didn't happen. It reminds me often of what could have happened and what God didn't allow to overtake me. Looking back now at the countless meaningless, empty and broken, relationships that scarred me deeply, I can't help but cry tears of joy. Today is my day of reckoning. Dark moments that played tricks within my mind and altered my past are still fresh in my memories, but they are no longer an open wound, but rather a beauty scar.

Praying that the attack on my life was over, I was excited to walk into my future. Feeling free from all the pain that I inflicted upon myself earlier in life, I was ready to move forward into my future. When greatness is upon your life, hell will attack with its greatest blow to take you out and put you under.

At the age of twenty, still feeling lost and afraid. I begin to search for the real clarity of my existence. My craving for desiring to simply be loved and admired begin to grow stronger. I begin to venture into relationships that devalued, devoured and detoured me from my real purpose in life. Since I chose not to feel that empty brokenness with positive enhancements, I remained empty. Emotionally unstable to balance myself, I moved quickly into what was obtainable. I wanted the void to go away. I didn't understand that my healing was deeper than an outer layer fix.

While on the journey of searching for me, I found him – Mr. Prince Charming. He had finally arrived. His appearance and lifestyle was a must and a big plus. Because I was so desperately empty, my heart was open without question. Mr. Charming had everything that any women could dream of: dark, tall, handsome, smart and had lots of money to spend. He drove a nice car, had swag and wore the latest labels that money could buy, but was birthed and born to cause havoc on my future. I was smitten with him because finally someone that was special, popular and amazing admired me.

He represented everything I desired to be, so I adored him even more. I was very careful in everything I did because I didn't want to lose him. I didn't want to be lonely anymore. He saw how I needed his presence and he used that to his advantage. Prince Charming began to play with my mind because I was open and allowed him to. His threats of leaving me only made me more erratically unstable. He knew what I needed and how I craved for his attention, which kept me emotionally dysfunctional for him.

Living a reckless life with him, I became pregnant thinking this would make everything perfect. Such a foolish and damaged girl I was. I was excited about revealing the amazing news to him. That was the evening that changed my life forever. I can remember screaming with excitement to him, "Congratulations, we are having a baby!" The look on his face was priceless, followed by the words that slowly came out of his mouth, "Meet me tomorrow at ten, I want to take you somewhere." Everything on the inside of me that morning was blank. I can't remember even if I said hello to him. We pulled into a Planned Parenthood Clinic, and he said firmly, "I will leave you if you keep it." My body went numb. It felt as if my heart stopped beating and everything was a blur. At that very second, my life, my dreams and hopes of keeping him was going up in flames.

The choice that I made left a hole in my heart. The feeling of emptiness was greater than that feeling of being alone. I hated him for the choice that I choose for him and the shame that I wore quickly. As I weep on the way home, I knew that wasn't the life for me. Thinking that he would stay was the greatest fairytale of them all. It was truly no Cinderella ending to this story.

Crushed and confused but determined not to give up on myself, I found my strength where I least expected it. I found strength within myself through the eyes of God. Under all of the ugly and damaged scars, I found hope and a story of victory was birthed.

The pain of my past haunted me daily in my other relationships. The hole that hindered my growth was deep and fierce. I grew up in the church and knew right from wrong, but my vision had gotten blurred because of my desire to seek after plastic emotions and unauthorized attachments. Knowing the truth and living by the truth are two totally different things. I was searching to be loved and validated, so the road to that meant giving up everything I had; my body, my values, and my future.

Exposing this battle brings so much healing to my yesterday. Why? Because my past does not dictate my present or my future. The pain of my yesterday has pushed me to pursue my purpose and has motivated me to mentor others to beat the odds of every distraction aimed towards them. Those were my mistakes then, but I am not her now. The battle of my past can no longer strangle or choke me out of my destiny testimony. Revelation 12:11(KJV), "And they overcame him by the blood of the Lamb, and by the word of their testimony."

Yes, today, you are an overcomer. You are forgiven. You are free. The shame of your past can no longer cause you to smother. Transparency brings freedom and freedom releases healing. You have suffered long enough from your mistakes, failures, and downfalls. The time is now, to make peace with your past and move bravely into the life that God has called for you. You have learned that your determination to live through it has made you stronger and given you strength to walk away from it. It is now your assignment to allow your story to change someone else's life. You have survived your lowest valley and now it is time to soar to the highest mountain.

Let the tears fall, you are now free to be the best that you can possibly be. Take a deep breath and exhale there is no going back now. Absolutely, you are good enough to live forward and be great. Every lie that you have heard since your childhood is now exposed and broken. The organ is playing at the funeral recession, the preacher is making the last decree over your past, "Ashes to ashes and dust to dust." Practice your Next Level Beautiful smile because greater days are not coming, they are here now. Now, it's your time, to walk into your purpose and conquer every battle that has been designed to deplete your destiny. Fast forward, no delays.

Prayer

Today, I close the book of my past. I cut the cord that held me bound. My past failures, relationships, mess ups, mishaps, mistakes and deliberate errors, are all behind me. Thank you, Lord, for allowing me to see the pain of my past. My past will no longer embarrass me, hurt me or haunt me. It is over and I have no hard feeling against it. I am truly free and I walk in my freedom through you. Today, I choose my future. In Jesus' name, Amen.

My Next Level: I Declare:

_____
_____
_____
_____
_____
_____
_____

Two

Battle of the Tongue

We all know someone that has been called a "big mouth." But are we really saying that their mouth is big, or that their tongue is out of control? Are we saying silently, "Can't they control themselves?" Proverbs 21:23 (KJV) tells us, "Whoso keepeth his mouth and his tongue keepeth his soul from troubles."

The tongue has the ability to bring the soul great troubles and bondage. Let's be honest; we have all said some things that we are not quite proud to own and wish we could take it back. Sometimes, you have been pushed to the edge and your words came back as a weapon in your defense. You must understand, "Life and death are in your mouth" (Proverbs 18:21).

Let's be completely transparent. You have often allowed the tongue to talk you out of promotions, marriages, relationships and so many other things because of the words that were chosen. Our tongue has ruined and delayed destiny moves because we have yet to tame it. I can personally remember saying things that my heart didn't feel, but my tongue felt it necessary to say. Isn't it quite funny that when you are angry and feel as if you want to "pop off," your tongue is always ready and available; egging you on and pushing you to say whatever it feels. Your tongue has no limitations. It's loose and wild and needs to be tamed.

The Bible tells us to guard our tongues. Why? Because if you don't, it will cause you to become injured both spiritually and physically. Spiritually, the scripture says to be slow to speak. Meaning you don't want words that have not been processed through your mind to jump off your tongue. You should think before you speak. It's better to look smart than to be proven not when you open up your mouth. Listen and observe then process and speak. Wisdom should flow out of your mouth and knowledge should be your friend. Also, physically you can be damaged because of your tongue.

If you're wondering how, try walking into a crowd of angry people and begin to tell them to shut-up. Physically, I don't believe you would make it out the room in one piece.

Your character is also connected to the battle of the tongue. People view you by what you say. The most amazing thing is this, once your heart is hurt because of what your tongue has said and done, your tongue seems to get quiet because the tongue knows it's time to apologize.

You must honestly get to a place where you take complete charge over your "big mouth." It can sometimes be viewed as a wild beast that must be muffled and tamed. You cannot allow your world to be framed by your ugly words. "Teach me, and I will hold my tongue: and cause me to understand wherein I have erred" (Job 6:24, KJV).

Your tongue is powerful. You must learn that you do not have to use your hands to cause damage, but a small dose of untamed tongue can be lethal. There have been instances that I had to confront my tongue to speak the truth. I had to tell my tongue, you will not speak lies and make up stories to make things sound more lavish and amazing. I had to learn that the truth was enough. I had to be at peace with saying a one line sentence and closing my mouth. Personally, I have always despised a quiet room and thought I had to create the conversation and keep things going. I had to study to be quiet.

One of the biggest mistakes you can make is accepting this unruly behavior of your tongue by saying, "It's just the way I am!" This lie must die. Let's be honest, the tongue will aim to find conflict and fault in everyone else, but it's your tongue that is operating in total dysfunction. Seriously, can we have a real conversation about life and death being in the power of the tongue? You have allowed one of the smallest parts of your body to rule over you.

If you think about it, some of your greatest hurts have come from another person's mouth. The emotional hurt from their tongue still plagues you from your childhood and has traveled with you into your adulthood. We learn behaviors from past experiences, whether good or bad and subconsciously begin to practice them. We become what hurt us if we are not careful to change it. What happened to you must stop with you. You must be real with yourself and the journey to Next Level Beautiful.

It's not a rude attitude that you were born with or a short temper that made you spin into a rage by using your tongue. It's simple…you must think before you speak. There are things that you must change to become better. It's no longer acceptable for your tongue to be a liar, manipulator, curser or trickster. That life is no longer who you are or what you want to be. It is impossible to heal what you hide.

In order to heal a physical sore that has been bleeding, you must uncover it and take the bandage off, clean it out and allow the fresh wind to begin the healing process. This is an inside job and you must search your heart to understand your tongue. Out of the heart flows the issue of life. Your tongue is obeying what's in your heart. The Bible says, "Create in me a clean heart" Psalm 51. You are spilling out what is residing on the inside of you.

Today, we stop the bleeding of the tongue and the hurt we caused others and ourselves, through our words. We surrender the hidden knife within our mouth and we exchange that weapon of bitterness for a cup of sweet words. It is not our intentions or desire to be ugly, mean or nasty with our tongue, so therefore, this is an easy process that starts with the phrase, "I choose beautiful." It no longer matters how other's will approach you and what they choose to say, you are in control of what comes out of your mouth. You are truly beautiful and your words are pleasant to hear. From this day forward, your words will reflect who you are.

Prayer

Father, today I admit that my tongue hasn't been pleasant or kind at times. I desire to speak pleasant words to those that come into my life and those that are involved in my future. I denounce every evil and nasty word that has grown to be a part of my future because of my past experiences. I am not what I allowed to come out of my mouth. I repent and move forward. For those that have left my life and that I have wronged with my ugly revengeful tongue because I was in pain and hurt, please forgive me now. I choose beautiful. Amen.

Next Level Beautiful

My Next Level: I Declare:

_____
_____
_____
_____
_____
_____
_____

Three

BATTLE OF THE FLESH

Okay, this chapter is about to get REAL. We are about to dig deep, uncover, expose, and uproot some things.

Through this chapter, you will not only expose your hidden secrets, but you will be healed from them. The Bible says, "Although I want to do good, evil is right there with me" (Romans 7:21, NIV). It's lurking, hiding, waiting and wanting you to give in. You live with it, wake up with it and even try to domesticate it. What is "it" you may ask? "It" is your flesh.

Outside of the battle of the tongue, your flesh is one of the most unruly members of your body. It has no limitations, no boundaries, and certainly no regrets. It wants to run free and be free at all times. The flesh seeks gratification and wants to please itself without restrictions. It's always hungry for its desires (food, sex, lying, cheating, stealing, or other compulsive behaviors) and will never be satisfied with the normal intake. Just think, right now... what is your flesh craving? What has caught your attention and made you lose focus?

What unauthorized behavior is calling your name and pushing you to yield to its control? Just like every other organ in the body, your flesh is alive, breathing and wanting to create its own agenda. It longs for things that are restricted, undisciplined and dangerous. Let's be real, at some point we have all quoted Matthew 26, "Watch and pray, that ye enter not into temptation: the spirit indeed is willing, but the flesh is weak. How many times have you said, "I can't explain what happened, everything went so fast?" Try explaining it by just stating, "My flesh is out of control!"

So many questions remain, how do we cage a creature that desires to indulge itself without limits or boundaries and how do we tame our flesh tendencies. The flesh reminds me of an illegal drug, it's only mission is to get you high and hooked. When you give in to the flesh it treats you like a junky looking for the next hit. The flesh has no respect for your title, position or status. It's brutal when the flesh is untamed and not buffered.

In order to triumph over the battle of your flesh, you must first begin by starving it. Romans 7:18 states, "For I know that in me that is, in my flesh dwelleth no good thing. For I have the desire to do what is right, but I cannot carry it out." If you want to win this battle, you must deprive yourself of the things your flesh crave. The objective is to kill it, not tame it.

I'm sure you heard the stories about zookeepers who fed the lions, tigers, and apes that were suppose to be "tamed?" But one day while servicing the animal, something strange happened and the "tamed" animal snapped and attacked the zookeeper. Believe it or not, this same concept applies to your flesh. If you just seek to tame it you will never be completely free from its desires and one day it will rise up against you.

You must take away the flesh kryptonite and deplete its power. 1Corinthians 10:13 clearly states, "No test or temptation that comes your way is beyond the course of what others have had to face." I have some amazing news, you are not fighting alone in the battle of the flesh.

Once you have positioned your mind to starve the flesh, expect every temptation to show up to try and feed it. The timing will be perfect, the person perfect, the atmosphere, location, and access, all perfect. But you must understand that starvation makes you stronger. Understand, you are coming out of the cage of flesh control. No longer will the flesh dictate when, where and who. God has given you the power to move forward and experience wholeness and peace within your flesh. You can do this. Remember, God will never let you down, he'll always be there to help you come through it. You will survive this.

Prayer

Today, I commit myself to living above the flesh. I crucify my desires and every craving that has tried to overtake me. I kill the flesh and all of its passions that control me and my appetite. What once controlled me must let me go. My inward desire is to be pleasing unto God. Not my will but your will be done in my life. God, you know my heart, you made me and I am your child. Numb every area that is screaming to be pleased. It isn't easy but with you it's possible. I submit to your plans for my life. In Jesus' name, Amen.

My Next Level... I Declare:

_____
_____
_____
_____
_____
_____
_____

Four

Battle of Temptation

Why is it so hard just to do the right thing and make the right choices for our life? Seriously, we wake up in the morning with our determination on high and our focus is geared to greatness. But along the way, temptation arrives. It arrives like a passenger on a plane that has a first class ticket. Romans 7:19, KJV says, "For the good that I would I do not: but the evil which I would not, that I do."

In laymen terms, I really want to do what's best for me but something on the inside of me continues to fight against me and push me to the other side. Have you ever asked the question, why? Let's define what temptation really is. Temptation is a fundamental desire to engage in short-term urges for enjoyment, that threatens long-term goals. Right when you begin to strive to do better and be better, temptation arrives. You try and avoid it and ignore it but it finds you. It entices you. It blinds you. It chases you. The smell, the music, the sunlight, a simple song reminds you of that great temptation that you once loved so much.

How do you take a test that you already have the answers to? The grading scale for the test of temptation is pass or fail. It's simple, you take the bait or you walk away. You jump or you sit! It's a test of character and integrity. Temptation toys with your mind and triggers your emotions. It entices your inner soul with questions of why not do it? What do you have to lose? Just this once and it will be okay. Temptation tricks you with pleasurable treats, flashing lights, and an endless night of passion and love. It feeds you with false destiny and hopes, empty promises and fulfillment.

Temptation is a tester. You are the target. Temptation plays dirty because it stands on quicksand. The moment you give in, you begin to sink because you didn't think that the aftermath would destroy everything you built.

Thoughts of, "How did I end back up in the same place again or why couldn't I just walk away," flood your mind. It's the battle of temptation we have all faced and failed, but today we will experience freedom from it. It played us last time, but now our focus has changed. Our heart has been strengthened and our mind has been renewed. We are no longer that broken child that just wants to be loved, we now love ourselves.

Yes, we wanted validation of our very existence, so temptation was there to lure us into that place of acceptance. So many bad choices, stupid mistakes, broken promises, lies, deception, and flawed friendships just because temptation was our driver and we were the rider.

Jesus fasted forty days and Satan showed up with bread, he refused to eat what he offered because destiny and purpose were his food. Just like Jesus, we can be strong and bold because we know the end result is the victory. You don't have to choose the tempter or the tester. Your value is greater than what they are tempting you with. It's time to rise. Rise up beautiful one. Tricks are for kids, and you have passed that test.

Put on your champion face because you are an overcomer. See it for what it really is, call it by its name. Scream to the top of your voice, "You can no longer tempt me. You cannot have my emotions, my thoughts or my reactions." You must address it and reject it. You have the power to take it by the throat and choke it to death. Yes, you must be brutally aggressive with it. You must become like an angry bear that has been in hibernation for a year and has rudely been awakened before the season is over.

Your total persona when facing temptation must be filled with rage and resentment because you know what it is there to do to you. Treat it like a prisoner that will never be granted parole. Inject a lethal dose of punishment towards it as you pull it down out of your life.

Temptation comes to sift you as wheat. But someone is pushing and praying for you, that your faith holds strong and you fail not. Just like Joseph in Genesis 37, he began to rise to the top of his destiny when everything that could have tempted him came directly at him. Potiphar, the captain of the palace guard, made Joseph the head of his household. However, Potiphar's wife was furious at Joseph for resisting her attempts to seduce (tempt) him and falsely accused him of attempted rape.

Let me give you a major news flash, you will be persecuted for not falling into the devil's snares, talked about and dismissed, but you will enjoy the benefits of not falling prey and living your truth. You must proclaim, "I will walk away from every distraction that my flesh is seeking that will eventually destroy me."

When you understand that you are so much more than what you have been settling for, you will begin to change your perspective and your decisions will be easier to walk away from one night thrills and quick releases. That life just isn't you anymore!

Prayer

I stand bravely before you Father, knowing that this battle is not easy. I am facing the hardest challenge of my life, and I need your strength. You said when I am weak you will be strong. I put my trust in you and allow you to work on my weaknesses. I give you my flesh that craves things that are not healthy for my life. I surrender all to you. My body, my mind and spirit belong to you.

My Next Level... I Declare:

_____
_____
_____
_____
_____
_____
_____

Battle of Fear

Afraid of heights. Afraid of spiders. Afraid of snakes. Afraid of failures. Afraid to meet new people. Afraid of being told "No." Afraid of dying prematurely. Afraid of losing everything. Afraid of not having enough. Afraid I will stay single. Afraid my marriage will never last. Afraid my ministry will never go forth. Afraid I will always be alone. Afraid of not having children. Afraid I won't be happy. The anxiety that accompanies fear can sometimes be greater than the fear itself. Feeling anxious is a normal reaction to stress, and everyone feels anxious from time to time.

Let's compare fear verses anxiety. Anxiety can be viewed positively when it helps motivate you to address a tense situation. But when we look at fear, it is defined as an unpleasant emotion caused by the belief that someone or something is dangerous, likely to cause pain or a threat. Fear is a feeling induced by a perceived danger or threat. Generally, when we think of fear we might equate it to anxiety, dismay, despair, horror, and worry. The Bible calls this, "the spirit of fear." Having the spirit of fear is very harmful. Proverbs 12:25 states, "Anxiety in a man's heart weighs him down, but a good word makes him glad."

One of my favorite scriptures: 2 Timothy 1:7 (KJV), "For God hath not given us the spirit of fear; but of power, and of love, and of a sound mind." You must operate on a level of a sound and solid mind. Fear will alter your thinking and push you to act out of character because you are afraid of the unknown.

Whether your fear was listed or not, the fact remains the same; there is something that all of us fear. Fear comes to incapacitate your mind with the ultimate goal of preventing you from moving forward. Seriously, after living afraid and being in fear, what do you have left? Life will continue to move forward with or without you. Fear is barbaric, savagely cruel and exceedingly brutal. Please understand, it is not okay to continue to live in a bubble that only produces fear and phobias, and only allows you to operate when it releases you.

Fear is tricky; it is a silent killer that torments you every time you consider doing something new. It reminds you of past failures, past hurts, and past mistakes. It comes to silence everything that you have dreamed of achieving. We have allowed things that haven't even happened to stop our progress because of fear. It's time to face what has been taunting you and see it for what it is.

Next Level Beautiful is calling you to come forward, but fear is punching you in the gut to stay silent. Which one will you say yes to? You are no longer frightened and afraid of what the future holds. The Bible says in Isaiah 43:19, "Behold I will do a new thing in you." Today, your new thing is blooming and flourishing. You are coming out of your cocoon and developing fresh new wings and moving quickly forward. You are not only fearless but fierce! God is developing boldness within you to walk into the next level of your life with confidence and courage. You are a force to be reckoned with. You walk by faith and not by fear. Square your shoulders and walk forward. Fear is not welcomed where you are going. The world is waiting on you to show up and take full control.

Prayer

Today, I release the battle of fear. I no longer choose to be afraid of the unknown. I choose to walk in confidence and courageousness. I no longer choose to operate as a frightened child. I am bold. I am fearless. I am a child of God. Fear has no place within my heart, in my life, in my destiny or in my now. I am free from fear.

Tawanda La'Shun Usher

My Next Level... I Declare:

_____
_____
_____
_____
_____
_____
_____
_____

Six

BATTLE OF THE SPIRIT

Restless. Weary. Torn. Sleepless. Tired. Tossing. Worried. Confused. Those are just a few things that will cause your spirit to be unsettled. It's time to address the unsettledness that you have harbored for too long. Can't sleep because your spirit is fighting? Can't move forward because your spirit is heavy? Today is the day that we address the battle of the spirit.

There have been so many times I have said, "It just doesn't feel right in my spirit." I'm sure you may have experienced the same, yet we continue to walk in that spirit. So many spirits that I can't list, but I want to guide this conversation and deal with the aspect of "settling the spirit."

Often it's too much going on and it's just too loud; too many decisions, too many distractions, too many choices, and too many voices. When you find yourself in a wave of noise, it's time to shut it down. It's imperative that you understand that chaos only gets louder. Like a radio with no knob on the volume, things turn up quickly. When you cannot settle your spirit, you are apt to live on the edge and in your feelings daily. We are emotional by trait, therefore when your spirit is going bananas you must know when to pull back and speak to it. You must ask God for a spirit of peace. A peace that causes every river to be calm and every mountain to be lowered. A peace that surpasses all understanding. Sometimes the peace you need is in the silence that you can't comprehend.

I would like to be transparent and share this experience with you. While in the middle of starting a childcare center in the month of November, during the off-season, I was preparing financial reports for the Certified Public Accountant and I literally lost it. The stress and the noise of the project had taken complete control over me. I remember driving in my garage and not being able to get out of the car. My entire body had shut down. Isn't it so amazing how warning comes before destruction. The day prior, God had been trying to get my attention, but I hadn't listened to the still, small voice. I disregarded His Spirit and took on the heaviness of life. I did it my way and the damage and disturbance weren't worth it.

So I say to you, calm your spirit. Listen to the voice of God. He is talking. He hears you clearly. Your spirit must be connected to His will. That's the peace that is required for your Next Level. You can't be loud all the time and expect to produce purpose, it's impossible. Because God speaks in a still small voice, you must decide to be at rest within your spirit with Him.

Trust me, things will come to uproot your peace and distract your spirit, but that's the beauty of the Next Level, knowing when you need to shut down. You must know when it's too loud. You must know when your spirit is troubled. You must know when to pull back and pray. Pulling back is not about being alone but being in touch with yourself. You are not moody, you just need a moment to reset and get your peace back period.

Take a minute and gather yourself for your next level. You will need that space to regroup and be at your best to conquer those unexpected roadblocks that will be thrown to detour and discourage you. Your spirit must remain on alert no matter what. You cannot allow your spirit to become contaminated with waste and spoiled goods. You are too valuable to be weighed down. Free your spirit of every heavy block, you were born to fly. A clear spirit will produce a purposeful destiny. Your mind, body, and spirit will congratulate you for allowing it to soar high.

Prayer

Lord, today I calm my spirit and rest. You know all things and I trust Your judgment. I pull down every sad, lonely, disturbing and ungodly spirit that has tried to attach itself to my life. I sever the cords that was sent to unsettle my thoughts and spirit. I shall be calm, I shall relax and I shall take control of my entire being. Nothing shall uproot me or make me anxious or worried. The spirit of peace is my portion and I embrace it with an open heart. In Jesus' name, Amen.

My Next Level: I Declare:

_____
_____
_____
_____
_____
_____
_____

Seven

BATTLE OF THE MIND

Shhhhhh listen, what is your mind saying right now? The mind is thinking, moving and gathering new thoughts and ideas, as well as the past, present and future experiences. Even things that have not yet happened, but the mind is already processing it.

Your mind is extremely powerful. Your mind is like an aircraft tower directing thousands of airplanes that are preparing for landings and takeoffs all while directing and maneuvering traffic on the ground and in the air. The mind is your air traffic controller for your body. It tells you where to go, how to get there, and what decisions to make once you arrive.

The mind is always on duty even when you are on vacation. It has no downtime or rest. It thinks without thinking. It is fueled by current thoughts, past experiences, good and bad emotions and is constantly gaining new information. Consider how it is possible to smell the wind and immediately have our mind take us back to the moment we smelled that very scent? Truly, we have underestimated the power of the mind. So how do you control something that never stops?

Just like a hungry child that is ready for dinner, your mind wants to be fed. It will feed off the good, the bad and the ugly, in order to keep growing. The mind is so powerful and strong that it will remind you of a past hurt that happened eight years ago and you still feel the pain like it happened yesterday. It is a battlefield and you must control it or it will lead you to a place of no return.

The mind needs to be guarded and directed. It must be guarded because it is very strong, but fragile. The brain is like a powerful computer that stores memories and controls how humans think and react. What you feed your mind will produce what it is fed. A junky mind produces negative thoughts and negative thoughts produce negative behaviors and negative behaviors breed an unhealthy lifestyle.

We must be willing to arrest every negative thought that comes to steal our joy, distract our focus and detour us from reaching our goals. Remember, negative thoughts keep us bound.

You should not be comfortable with allowing the negative to take residence within your mind. You eliminate these negative thoughts by redirecting your mind with pleasant and powerful engaging thoughts. Think on things that are lovely and pure and of a good report. So, what are you feeding your mind? The Bible says in Romans 12:12, "Do not conform to the pattern of this world but be transformed by the renewing of your mind. Then you will be able to test and approve what God's will is – his good, pleasing and perfect will of God."

It's transformation time! You must continuously deposit positive thoughts into your mind, which will affect your actions and emotions. You will never be at your best by having a mind that is polluted with thoughts that do not enhance your purpose. The mind is so incredibly amazing and it wants to be expanded, it wants to grow.

When you decide to remove the negative thoughts that are so easy to pick up, you must replace that space with creative positive things: pick up a new art class, go back to school, create a new vision board for your life. Remember, you have years of experience that you have allowed negative thinking to enter into your head-space. So don't get discouraged when you hit a bump in the road. Don't be hard on yourself but encourage yourself by saying; "I will think positive, I will feed myself with things that are beautiful."

You have the ability to think on positive things that will bless your atmosphere and encourage your future. Stop allowing the negative to become your reality. Overcoming the battle of the mind is imperative in pursuing your purpose and destiny. Your support group will be essential to your forward movement. Surround yourself with people that are motivated and excited about life.

Negative thinkers seek minds that are compatible. It's time to weed out and filter everything that is not healthy to developing and producing a positive mind. You will not be able to obtain a balanced life by wavering. Things change when you change the way you think. You can't afford to be unstable and double-minded (James 1:8). You must be solid and ready for your Next Level without having second thoughts about it.

The Bible encourages us to arrest every evil imagination that rises up. Make a decision to arrest your mind, your thoughts and actions today. Pull down every stronghold, every dark thought and every weakening action that has come against your mind and begin to move forward. It will take repetition and practice to build up positive thinking and you have exactly what it takes to prevail. Trust me, the more you feed your mind with good, pleasant and powerful thoughts, the more it will regurgitate what you have given it. When you are passionate about moving forward, nothing can stop your progress. Every negative thought must bow down and be demolished. You absolutely have the power to win the battle of the mind. Shhhhhhhh, listen, what is your mind saying now?

Prayer

Father, in the name of Jesus I pray now that the battle of the mind is being removed now. My mind is being washed and purified. I cannot be my best with a crippled mind-frame. Lord, only you can transform my mind and teach me daily how to renew it. Please forgive me for living beneath your promises. My mind is washed and my spirit is open. I am ready to move forward. Let nothing disturb my elevation to Next Level Beautiful in Jesus' name, Amen.

My Next Level: I Declare:

_____
_____
_____
_____
_____
_____

Eight

Battle of Insecurity

What does it mean to walk in insecurity? First, let's define the word. Insecurity, or the act of being insecure, means feeling vulnerable, lacking confidence or feeling as if oneself is in danger, according to Webster's Dictionary online. Although we have our own fixed idea about what we think insecurity looks like, it actually manifests itself in various forms.

Some people feel as if the world is watching their every move and are constantly judging them or measuring them up. Others may walk in insecurity by judging their physical appearance or pointing out their flaws. They may say, "my height is too short, my skin is too dark, my feet are too big. If I was a little smarter, brighter, lighter, bolder I would be much better. I would be much further ahead than where I am now."

I can remember standing in the mirror and not having any kind words to say about myself. Truth be told, there was nothing wrong with me, but there was something wrong with the mirror I was looking into. The mirror was all wrong and needed to be adjusted or replaced. It was flawed and off centered, chipped and unreliable.

The mirror of insecurity shows you what you're not and can't become. It never compliments what you are and what you're striving to be. That old mirror is not your friend but your foe. It aims to pull your spirit down and leave you with years of disappointment. Insecurity taunts your progress and aims to throw shade and stop your growth. The mirror of insecurity is not positive but negative.

So today, I am giving you the right to pick up that baseball bat and swing away at that flawed mirror. Your days of insecurity are over. Feeling as if the world is watching your every move, being worried and consumed by what others think or feel about you, having to dummy down, are all ending now.

Mirror, mirror on the wall who's the fairest of them all? Since the mirror refuses to answer, I will answer for you. You have always been that girl. The mirror just didn't know it. It was too busy pointing out your flaws and not appreciating your strengths. The mirror of insecurity desired your attention but spoke dissension to you. Now that you have crashed that mirror, it's time to create one that will allow you to embrace every part of you.

You are good enough, pretty enough, and smart enough. Liar, liar the mirror is on fire. You have broken what has tried to break your confidence. You are fearfully and wonderfully made. Darling, you are beautiful. Tell your mirror you no longer need its services. The mirror that you now see, comes from within you. Reprogram the way you process yourself and speak beautiful things that push you forward.

Embrace your beauty and enhance who God has called you and created you to be. Psalms 139:14 "I will praise thee; for I am fearfully and wonderfully made; Wonderful are Your works, and my should knows it very well." There is no question about it, God created only the best when He created you.

Prayer

Father, help me to overcome my inner insecurities that often plague my mind and spirit. Help me to accept things that I cannot change and embrace the differences that I see within myself. Let me know that you have made me perfectly and I am thankful for who I am and who I am becoming. Lord, cleanse my thoughts of me and show me what you see. You see beauty and you see perfection because you made me the way I am.

Next Level Beautiful

My Next Level... I Declare:

_____
_____
_____
_____
_____
_____
_____

Nine

BATTLE OF PEOPLE

Let's talk! Honestly, do you really think they care about what you are wearing or thinking about them? Yes, the Joneses. We need to first find out why we are so fascinated with keeping up with the Joneses. Who are these people that don't even know you exist? Why do we consistently measure our validation by their standards on what's hot and what's not? What is in season or out of fashion?

We need to have a sit-down, real-time chat. What is the benefit for trying to keep up with the Joneses and be a part of their lives? What is the reward, the prize or the position you will receive? We are not just talking about the Joneses, but we are uncovering a covenant spirit that longs to live above the line and above others. It aims to shine and be the top dog and the leading person in the room. It is a dangerous scenario to seek after the Joneses. Let me explain why.

What you have built around the Joneses will come to a complete halt and eventually crash. Trust me, this is how the steps of the ladder crumbles and falls. The first thing that will happen is totally innocent, the way you view the Joneses through eyes of admiration. We admire them because they are cutting-edge, trend-setters and trailblazers. We esteem their passion to pursue, conquer and achieve great things. They exemplify a tenacity and zeal about themselves that others can't deny. We praise them for setting the bar high and living well. We compliment them, smile with them, and visit with them; and soon after that something begins to shift from admiring them to wanting to be them.

We no longer allow them to be the only ones in the room that represent the attitude of success and power. You study them and from there, you copy them because they can no longer exist in that space alone because you crave that position. Without delay, you shift into that position and seize the moment.

Immediately, we go and purchase that look that they have, the shoes that they wear, clothes they display, the car they drive and the type of house they purchased. You struggle to stay relevant by fighting eviction notices monthly. You work harder to rent what they have purchased with cash. While they are buying cars, you are borrowing them. The Joneses dress nice but it's all paid in cash while your credit card for the same items comes with twenty-two percent interest. You are paying for winter clothes on your bill in the summer time. Nothing makes sense in your life because you are choosing to live a lie that will never be the truth. Your desire to live better and have better is justified, but your motives are mostly distorted. You can never be at your best by being a carbon copy of someone else.

After you admired the Joneses then you want to be them. The final stage is that once you can't achieve their success, you begin to hate them. This stage is very dangerous and extremely evil and must be rooted out rather than controlled. Hate is a powerful word and I use this word loosely because it travels with companions. Greed, envy, and jealousy are linked to the last phase of the Battle of People. You will not move forward working in the operation of any of these destiny breakers. Greed is defined as intense and selfish desire for something, especially wealth and power. Envy is a feeling of discontented or resentful longing aroused by someone else's possessions, or qualities. The combination of greed and envy will cause major casualties once they collide. It's not healthy to desire what is not meant for your future. It's not always about the people, but maybe this is about you.

Truth be told, we always say we don't know how or what the Joneses did to get what they have. Can we assume that the

Joneses have what they have because they have positioned themselves to reap the harvest? Could it be possible the Joneses have invested wisely and can now enjoy their labor of seed planting? Could it be possible that the Joneses are givers and that they believe they are the lender and not the borrower. Could it be that in their private time they are giving God the glory for everything that they have in their possession? Could it be that they have educated themselves on IRA's and Investing Bonds, sat down with their financial investor and created a wealth of businesses, and this is the residual of their years of business plans, profits, and income reports, and lowering their debt ratio on the personal side to invest larger on the business side? Yes, could it be?

So stop trying to be like someone that doesn't even know you exist. Set up a meeting with the Joneses and ask them how they achieved so much. Please understand, there is nothing wrong with a few higher priced desires here and there, but let's be real, it's time to buy smart.

What do you gain by wearing red bottoms, Gucci and Prada shoes, when your paycheck doesn't cover the purchase? This is your awakening party! Your life will immediately begin to shift once you get the revelation of beating the Battle of People. When you wake up and begin to understand, that after spending all that hard cash, a compliment is your reward and that doesn't pay the bills. Lord deliver us from people, people opinions, people thoughts, people actions and people ways.

We give too much energy trying to prove to the Joneses that we have arrived. Honestly, they are busy building a dynasty. Too much energy on all the wrong things that will never push you to live forward. Our focus is shifting from pleasing people to becoming a better person.

You are born for better and you have everything that you need to be the best you. It's not what you have but who you are and what you have inside you. Look deep inside yourself and birth out the beauty that has been dormant for so long. Take off the shoes that no longer fit you, for your next level is calling you forward. Where you are going you will need shoes of excellence and integrity. Shoes that guide and lead you into your purpose.

You are getting ready to walk into new places, doors of which fabulous labels, titles and brand names will not open. You are original and there is none more beautiful than you, not just your outside beauty, but your beautiful kind heart that you wear like an expensive Chanel bracelet. Be comfortable with who you are called to be. You are a royal priesthood, very delightful and blessed. People will be happy to get to know the real you. Go ahead, try it on. You will love the authenticity.

Prayer

Today, I will not be controlled by what others have or what I don't have. I will walk in the security of knowing who God has called me to be. I will master and build on the gifts that God has given me. I have changed my focus and this will change my life. I am walking forward in Jesus' name.

My Next Level... I Declare:

_____
_____
_____
_____
_____
_____
_____

Ten

Battle of Poverty

The story of robbing Peter to pay Paul stops today. I start this chapter by arresting the spirit of lack and poverty and the need to walk in the level of not enough. I speak to the spirit of Pharaoh to unchain and release those that have a true desire to prosper and excel. We stand on the back of bondage, slice it from the neck and demolish it.

The need to borrow from others, but wear Jordan's, and carry the latest iPhone is over. The desire to produce crumbs after pushing eighty hours of work in one week is over. We bury and burn the burden of debt and generational curses of money issues. The attitude of, let me spend it because I won't be able to take it when I die, is over. We gut out the word poor from our vocabulary and refuse to speak it or write it any longer.

Today, we start a revival in our finances and call wealth forth from the north, south, east and west. We stir the winds to blow fresh money into our hand and household. We speak an ocean of increase to flood our atmosphere, bank account, and surroundings. You were born to receive wealth and riches. You absolutely can handle multiple streams of income and inheritances that are willed to you.

I speak not one bank account, but a plethora of accounts with your name on it. You are not below the poverty line but live above average. You were not born on the wrong side of the tracks and dealt a bad deck of cards.

You should be celebrating right now because this chapter is about to break the chain of bondage off of your life. Once you know that you are called to be a giant killer in the world, nothing else matters. Money has to obey its Master. You must start now, yes right now, and declare, "I have more than enough." If you can be trusted with what you already have, you will be given more.

Are you truly ready to live in abundance and more? Don't answer yes so quickly. Let's first start by taking a peek at your bank account statement and see what your life is saying. Line by line will show what your desire, passion, and purpose support. Seriously, I will give you five minutes to grab that bank statement. Okay, you have it? Now, look at it. You should see destiny spending or frugal spending. You should see traces of your spending that displays and reflects your habits. Wait, is that McDonald's throughout the itemized bank statements? You should have stock with them the way you support them. Should I call you a part owner, business partner or just a plain groupie of the establishment? Trust me, someone is very appreciative of your regular support. Do me a favor and at least ask for a hat or t-shirt because you have earned it.

You have read enough lullaby stories and drunk enough fake fantasies. It's time to push pass the poverty mentality and experience true prosperity. Real revelation happens when you acknowledge you are on a ride to never-never-land because of the way you are choosing to live without regard. It's not that you don't make the money and earn a good wage; it's what you are doing with what you are receiving.

Wise up soldier and put that burger down. Aren't you full of meat that doesn't satisfy you? Living with a poverty mindset can keep you on a broken and relentless cycle. You have the power to break it off of your life. Open your eyes and see where you have thrown away your money through your lack of management. Do you see it? Now take full control of it.

The Bible says in Ecclesiastes 10:19 "Money is the answer for everything." Yes, this is true but you must first analyze what answer you are seeking. We tend not to respect money for what it was sent to do. We allow our habits to be the answer and money just supports it. Once you change your perspective of how money is supposed to answer all of your essentials, it will begin to work for you.

For example, the government system by law must provide housing for those that qualify and live under the poverty line. They pick those that have low or no income. They build beautiful apartments with the same qualities as regular homes or apartments. Because of some of the mentalities of those that move into the housing or projects, they treat it as if it's nothing special. Why? It's because their view of where they are has not changed.

You can't control what's around you, but you can control what's been given to you. In other words, the ghetto has the potential to be the best area ever, but the mindset of some will not let it be great. Your money has the potential to be amazing, great and grow. It's tired of being spent on things that don't matter. Your money wants to be the answer to everything. You are not letting your money do what it was created to produce. I have a question for you, a self-financial exam, "Are you the culprit or the root of your money problems?" Are you pushing an agenda that your money doesn't want to participate in and you are forcing it to be a part? If money was created to answer all things, it's time for you to think and value your money more. Plan now by creating opportunities for yourself to win with your finances.

Embrace the now! You should feel empowered enough to change your spending habits and pursue more positive methods of moving forward. You have what it takes to experience abundance with your money and live a life of overflow and fulfillment. Nothing is stopping you. You got this. I'm pushing for you. A debt free life is where you are now heading. Get ready to see it come to pass.

Prayer

Today, we stand in agreement concerning our finances and bring them into order. We will no longer just spend because we can, but we will save because we want to get ahead. God, we are grateful for every penny that you have released within our hands. Let us value our money more and aim to be farther than we have ever been within the next few months. We decree and declare our Next Level Beautiful be released now. In Jesus' name, Amen.

Next Level Beautiful

My Next Level… I Declare:

_____
_____
_____
_____
_____
_____
_____

Eleven

BATTLE OF PROCRASTINATION

You have delayed long enough. You promised yourself you would get around to pushing those projects forward. You go out, get the blank book, the sewing machine, buy the computer program, enroll in the class, purchase the pots and pans, buy the canvas board and paint and then six months later, you notice the items are in the same bag you bought them in.

Your money is exhausted with you starting projects and then storing them away. Everyone has heard of your big dreams and promises but the vision is still in the bag. The phone calls and conference calls of working your dreams, passions, and vision are all in the bag and in a closet next to the garage.

When is enough, enough? You have enlisted others to buy into your pipe dream and make the dream a part of their lives. They have started leading your vision that was originally your baby to carry. What happened to the scripture to write the vision, make it plain and then run with it? Why have you stopped running? Where have you hidden your running shoes? Have you cashed them in for another impotent empty dream and promise?

What exactly were your intentions when you initially thought about the big dream that was so deep inside of you? What was the purpose behind your passion for the project? Let's be real, it cost you something to even talk about the startup. What made you give up so easy on seeing it come to pass? Habakkuk 2:2, "Write the vision; and make it plain." Congratulations, you have completed part one of that verse. But you forgot that in order for it to work, you must "Run with it!"

Please stop pulling people into this balloon that is full of empty promises. I will be the first to admit and confess, that this use to be me. Yes indeed. I loved starting projects and getting the fancy things that went with each project. It was so much fun. I would lay out everything on the table and sort the items out, but then the thrill would leave. The spark and passion for the project would fade. The products purchased would pile high in the closet. The thrill to spend and not produce the project became a bad habit within my life. I had felt no dedication or loyalty to my purchase. Dedication is the quality of being committed to a task or purpose. What's very interesting, you have what it takes and the initial push to start projects but your delivery never develops.

You must raise your level of tenacity to next level approval. It will cost you time and endless hours of dedication and focus. Just like the bird that aims to build a nest, it is imperative for the bird to first seek the items that are needed to complete the task. Just because the bird desires a nest it doesn't just happen. It takes collecting sticks and positioning them a certain way for mobility and comfort. Your project and plan will not just happen, impossible.

Your plan must be crystal clear and very precise. It must be a blueprint of excellence that you completely believe in. Don't be surprised, everyone will not support and push your projects. Because of your previous procrastination track record, you will have to rebuild your foundation again. It will not be easy because of the distractions that will be presented, but you must not lose focus. You must buckle down and stay on the road that leads you to success.

Maybe you have written the vision and it's plain but you have recently hit a snag in the road. You must not be discouraged or lose your strength in the process. You must seek out powerful people that have walked before you and have beat the odds of delays. You are not on this journey alone.

Allow your drive and passion to continue to thrust you forward. You are truly a visionary, problem solver, innovator, creator, designer, and dreamer. You have witty and amazing ideas that could possibly make history. Imagine this, your vision could be featured in the next issue of Forbes magazine.

You must stop and take charge of the spirit of delay and procrastination that has lived so comfortably in your life. Someone is waiting patiently for your bright idea to show up and shake the nation. You have been delayed long enough and today you will regain the momentum that will propel you forward to completion. You have the power to produce and push out passionate projects. Let's get moving; you have the next biggest idea that will crack the ceiling and make history. Your design team is waiting in the board room for your arrival. It is your time. Write it down. Make it plain. Run with it!

Prayer

Father, today I pray that You will redirect my thoughts to focus on things that will push me forward. I admit I have operated in procrastination and excuses. Today, I pick up the projects that I have neglected and I begin to work them with great passion. I will not just start new ventures but I will make them adventures and enjoy completing them. I am the next big idea and I embrace it now.

My Next Level... I Declare:

_____
_____
_____
_____
_____
_____
_____
_____

Twelve

BATTLE OF THE FUTURE

Although we have differences that set us apart as individuals, one thing that we can all agree is that we have all faced some of the toughest battles in our life. Whether your battles are from the past or you are currently in one, we have yet to face the battle of the future.

We may not want to admit it, but most of us battle with our future. It's just something about not knowing what lies ahead that makes us very anxious. Our anxiety not only surfaces because we are unsure about our next phase in life, but also because we have no idea how we will successfully get there. Yes, the scripture speaks of an expected end…but what exactly does that end look like?

Let's be honest, everyone wants to know what the future holds. We talk about our future but sometimes planning for the future causes us anxiety. The uncertainty of what we should do next causes us to panic with anticipation. We begin asking questions like: Will I ever finish college? Will I ever get married and have children? Will I have enough money for retirement? Will I lose my job security and become homeless? Will I ever reach the greatest potential in my life time? These are all real questions that you at some point may face.

When transitioning to the Next Level, we have to be careful not to turn our anticipation into desperation. We can not become so desperate to discover our future by turning to ungodly and unqualified sources such as tarot cards, astrologists, and palm readers. Your future must be protected at all cost. These sources may appear harmless or even sometimes done in fun, but can cause more confusion and still leave you questioning. Let's address some of the fears of approaching the future. First, we must understand that fear is not real. It comes to rob you and hijack your future and stop you from moving forward. Fear comes to incapacitate your movement and cripple you from reaching your destiny. Moving forward, I want you to think of Fear as an acronym for False Evidence Appearing Real. Here are two key actions that can assist you in overcoming your fear and help you prepare for your future:

1. Equip yourself with valid and applicable information.

Your future is going to happen as long as you are still living so approaching it with great positivity and planning will give you a better chance of success. Truth be told, worrying only causes conflict and panic. You must settle your emotions concerning the future and embrace the planning process. If you have dreams of being a successful business owner or you hope to purchase a home one day, there is a certain amount of information you must obtain. For example, you may need to gather information on how to gain wealth, how to properly save, and learn how to invest your money.

2. Ground yourself in your current state.

It is essential to assess where you are in the present to understand where you will be in the future. Start taking a personal inventory of who you are currently, which includes but isn't limited to your current mental, emotional, and spiritual health, your current place of residence, and your financial status. The Scriptures state: Philippians 4:11, "Not that I speak in respect of want; for I have learned, in whatsoever state I am, to be content." Being content is not settling but appreciating your present circumstances.

During this season of transition and waiting, start to align yourself with "destiny pushers." These are people called to assist you while navigating through this battle. By connecting with those that are called and qualified to be a part of your destiny, you will begin to experience and understand the process. Please note, everyone is not called to be a part of the shift in your life, so do not be surprised if some of your "destiny pushers" are new connections.

Your future will be amazing as you plan and prepare with great excitement and expectation. Get ready because it is going to require a higher level of readiness and commitment. You must be 100% invested and focused; body, mind, and spirit. Be careful not to adopt the syndrome of YOLO, "You Only Live Once." Remember that living frivolously and without a plan can cost you more than you can afford in the long run.

Therefore, you must be steadfast when approaching the future. Jeremiah 29:11 clearly states, "I know what I'm doing. I have it all planned out – plans to take care of you, not abandon you, plans to give you the future you hope for." You are about to embark upon some of the greatest days of your life. No worries, no panic, only positivity and a plan for success. Be intentional. Be strategic. Your planning will pay off with interest.

Prayer

Today, I embrace my future. It is bright and it is calling me by name. I can no longer fuel fear and detours that have crippled my destiny. I know your plans for my life are great. I pray now that those that are assigned to my life will begin to show up. My health, wealth, and life are lining up to exceed my expectations. I am excited about my future plans and ready to work towards building a better life. In Jesus' name, Amen.

My Next Level... I Declare:

_____
_____
_____
_____
_____
_____
_____

Final

BLESSED BEYOND THE BATTLE

Put your graduation hat on, along with your robe of excellence and medal of honor. You have pushed through each battle and now you are stamped with the seal of Next Level Beautiful.

You have surprised the world with your strength and tenacity. The battles that were after you could not hold you down or break you apart. Everything that has tried to manipulate your destiny has made you stronger. Your strength is undeniable and cannot be understood by many. Your mistakes, failures and mishaps can no longer label you and define who you are. You have pressed through the ugliest days of your life, and now you are ready to experience authentic and genuine beauty. Beauty that goes beyond the skin and comes from the heart.

Nobody expected you to be at this amazing level of success because of all the battles that you had to face. The lies, threats, pain, and pressure that you endured have not caused you to hide but you have been washed and reborn to be presented as better. You have emerged with new hope and dreams that were lost and forgotten because of the pain and pressure of the battles you fought through. Your determination is a force to be reckoned with. They won't be able to sleep on your progress because it will be hard to keep track of the blessings you are about to walk into.

Amos 9:13 MSG, "Yes indeed, it won't be long now." GOD'S Decree. "Things are going to happen so fast your head will swim, one thing fast on the heels of the other. You won't be able to keep up. Everything will be happening at once and everywhere you look, blessing!" Because you did not quit and you didn't throw in the towel, even when you felt like it, God is getting ready to release perpetual blessings over your life. The minute you tell him thank you, the next blessing will be arriving. Instead of the *Battles* you will be receiving the *Blessings*.

The scars that made you cry will now be the story that highlights your victory. Take a quick glance in the mirror and smile. You have made it through some of the most challenging times of your life and you have survived them all because you are still standing. Please understand, this is not about people seeing and acknowledging your victories but this is about you embracing your life.

To every battle, every person, every problem, every downfall that has hurt you, knowingly or unknowingly, they are forgiven. You cannot be Next Level Beautiful harboring and sheltering pain. Not only do you forgive them, but you must forgive yourself. You have learned and grown from each experience that has manifested in your life. Let it go and move forward.

Let go of all the lies that have plagued you physically, mentally and emotionally. The battles of your yesterday can no longer immobilize your healing because you are more than a conqueror. You are a Champion that is positioned to pursue what God has intended for your life. Isaiah 61:1, "Arise, shine, for your light has come, and the glory of the LORD rises upon you."

Get ready to celebrate because your private tears can now be displayed as a public smile. There's no more fear in moving forward because your silent pain has been exposed and the beautiful voices of victory have risen. Can you hear it? The music is playing. They are calling your name to walk across the "Next Level" stage. You are no longer broken in pieces but beautifully whole. God has given you a clean heart and has delicately and so uniquely renewed your spirit. You are truly unbreakable.

Next Level Beautiful

As you enter into your Next Level Beautiful, embrace the "Beauty of Transition" with confidence and an open heart. You are blossoming not with anticipation but with great expectation. Get ready to journey further than you have before and experience the best of your life. You have indeed possessed beauty beyond pain.

Prayer

Father, as we close one chapter within our lives and walk into the next, we say, "thank you." It certainly has not been easy, but it has been worth it. Everything that I have been through has made me better. Some things have hurt me deeply but I am walking in my complete healing and moving forward. Give me the strength that is needed to understand my steps of transition from my ashes to beauty. I am grateful that I have identified all the battles that I have struggled with but survived. During my process of transition allow me to embrace where I am mentally, physically, spiritually and emotionally, and position me to win while I prepare for my destiny shift. In Jesus' name, Amen.

About the Publisher

Let *Life to Legacy* bring your story to literary life! We offer the following publishing services: manuscript development, editing, transcription services, ghost-writing, cover design, copyright services, ISBN assignment, worldwide distribution, and eBook conversion.

We make the publishing process easy. Throughout production, we keep the author informed every step of the way. Even if you do not have a manuscript, that's not a problem for us. We can ghost-write your book from audio recordings or legible handwritten documents. Whether print-on-demand or trade publishing, we have packages to meet your publishing needs. At *Life to Legacy*, we take the stress out of becoming a published author.

Unlike other *so-called* publishers, we do more than just print books. Our books and eBooks are distributed to book buyers, distributors, and online retailers throughout the world – this is real publishing! Call us today for a free quote.

Please visit our website
www.Life2Legacy.com

or call us
877-267-7477

Send e-mail inquiries
Life2Legacybooks@att.net

www.ingramcontent.com/pod-product-compliance
Lightning Source LLC
Chambersburg PA
CBHW031209090426
42736CB00009B/851